Overview *My Little Fish*

A pet fish swims around its bowl.

Reading Vocabulary Words	**High-Frequency Words**
beside	*my*
inside	*is*
diver	*the*

Building Future Vocabulary

* These vocabulary words do not appear in this text. They are provided to develop related oral vocabulary that first appears in future texts.

Words:	*top*	*gold*	*float*
Levels:	Yellow	Purple	Silver

Comprehension Strategy
Drawing conclusions

Fluency Skill
Emphasizing words in boldfaced type

Phonics Skill
Consonant blend: *sh*
(fi<u>sh</u>, <u>sh</u>ell)

Reading-Writing Connection
Writing about how to care for a pet

Home Connection
Send home one of the Flying Colors Take-Home books for children to share with their families.

Differentiated Instruction
Before reading the text, query children to discover their level of understanding of the comprehension strategy — Drawing conclusions. As you work together, provide additional support to children who show a beginning mastery of the strategy.

Focus on ELL
- Model *inside* and *beside* using a small object and a bag or box. Say *It is* beside *the bag* and *It is* inside *the bag*.

- Repeat these actions several times, with children saying either *beside* or *inside*.

T1

Using This Teaching Version

1. Before Reading

2. During Reading

3. Revisiting the Text

4. Assessment

This Teaching Version will assist you in directing children through the process of reading.

1. **Begin with Before Reading** to familiarize children with the book's content. Select the skills and strategies that meet the needs of your children.

2. **Next, go to During Reading** to help children become familiar with the text, and then to read individually on their own.

3. **Then, go back to Revisiting the Text** and select those specific activities that meet children's needs.

4. **Finally, finish with Assessment** to confirm children are ready to move forward to the next text.

1 Before Reading

Building Background

- Write the word *fish* on the board. Read it aloud. Have children share what they know about fish as animals in nature, as pets, and as food for people. Correct any misinformation.

- Introduce the book by reading the title, talking about the cover illustration, and sharing the overview.

Building Future Vocabulary
Use Interactive Modeling Card: Sentence Maker

- Introduce the word *float*. Have children take turns asking and answering "Does _____ float?" List items that float and those that do not.

- Have children make up other sentences using the word *float*.

Introduction to Reading Vocabulary

- On blank cards write: *beside, inside,* and *diver*. Read them aloud. Tell children these words will appear in the text of *My Little Fish*.

- Use each word in a sentence for understanding.

Introduction to Comprehension Strategy

Use Interactive Modeling Card: Questions and Answers Chart

- Explain that people use what they know, what they see, and what they read to draw conclusions.
- Tell children they will be drawing conclusions as they read *My Little Fish*.
- Introduce the Questions and Answers Chart. Tell children to raise their hands when they want to add a question to the chart.

Introduction to Phonics

- Write *sh* on the board. Say /sh/. Have children repeat /sh/.
- Together read the sentence on page 8. Tell children to raise their hands when they hear a word that ends with /sh/. (**fish**) Then have children locate the word on the page. Repeat for initial /sh/. (**shell**)
- Brainstorm words with final and initial /sh/. List these words in separate columns on chart paper and underline the *sh* in each word.

Modeling Fluency

- Write on the board the sentence "Here it is," writing the word *here* in heavy, bold letters. Read aloud the sentence, emphasizing *here*.
- Discuss how dark or heavy letters are used for emphasis. Discuss how boldfaced type is used in different kinds of texts. Show examples of boldfaced type in other books, if available.

2 During Reading

Book Talk

Beginning on page T4, use the During Reading notes on the left-hand side to engage children in a book talk. On page 16, follow with Individual Reading.

During Reading

Book Talk

- Have children look at the title page illustration. Have them point to and name the things in the picture. (fish, bowl, table, boat)

- Say *What do you think this book will be about?* (a little fish that lives in a bowl; what the fish does)

➡ *Turn to page 2 – Book Talk*

My Little Fish

Revisiting the Text

Future Vocabulary

- Direct children to look at the cover illustration. Ask *What color is the fish?* (yellow, gold) *What kind of fish is it?* (yellow fish, gold fish) Elicit from children the word *gold*.

- Say *A long time ago, people used a metal called gold as money. Today some jewelry is made from gold. Can you think of things that are made of gold?* (wedding rings, earrings)

- Have children make up sentences with the word *gold*.

Now revisit pages 2–3

1

During Reading

Book Talk

- Ask *Where is the fish?* (in the water, near the rock, to one side of the rock) *The fish is beside the rock.*
- Have children point to and name the parts of the fish: eyes, mouth, fins, tail.

Turn to page 4 – Book Talk

My little fish is beside the rock.

Revisiting the Text

Future Vocabulary
- Point out the air bubbles on page 3. Say *These bubbles are floating to the surface. Air is lighter than water, so the bubbles rise.*

Now revisit pages 4–5

During Reading

Book Talk

- Read the sentence on page 4, emphasizing *beside*. Have children locate the word *beside* on this page. Ask *What is another way to say that without using the word beside?* (The fish is next to the boat.)

- **Comprehension Strategy** Ask *How big is the boat? Is it big enough to hold a person?* (No, it's little; it's a toy boat.) Discuss how children came to that conclusion. (by comparing it to the size of the little fish, by remembering the title page and that the boat is *inside* a small fish bowl)

Turn to page 6 — Book Talk

My little fish is beside the boat.

Revisiting the Text

Future Vocabulary

- Say *In this picture, the boat is on the bottom of the bowl. But where do you usually see boats?* (on *top* of the water) *Do boats float?* (yes) Refer back to the list you made earlier about things that *float*.

- Discuss multiple meanings of *float* as a verb and a noun. Ask *Does anyone use a float or floaties when he or she goes swimming?*

- Ask *Has anyone ever had an ice-cream float? An ice-cream float is made with ice cream and a soft drink. How do you think it got its name?* (The ice cream *float*s on *top* of the soft drink.)

Now revisit pages 6–7

During Reading

Book Talk

- Ask *What are the bubbles in the picture?* (air) Explain that fish need oxygen from the air to survive. *What body part do fish use to get the oxygen they need?* (gills)

- Have children locate the word *beside* on this page. Ask *What is the fish beside on page 7?* (a plant)

- Continue to add questions to the Questions and Answers Chart as they arise.

Turn to page 8 – Book Talk

My little fish is beside the plant.

Revisiting the Text

Future Vocabulary

- Ask *Do you think the plant in the fish bowl is real or plastic?* (real, plastic) *We can't really tell.* Explain that some real plants grow on land, and some grow underwater. Tell children that some plants, called water lilies, have leaves and flowers that float on the water.

Now revisit pages 8–9

During Reading

Book Talk

- Have children find the picture on page 8. Say *Look at the word at the end of the sentence. It is next to the picture. Use the picture to help you read the word.*

- **Phonics Skill** Say *The word* shell *begins with /sh/. What can you see in the picture that ends with /sh/?* (fish) Remind them of the /sh/ word lists you made earlier in the lesson.

➔ *Turn to page 10 – Book Talk*

My little fish is beside the shell.

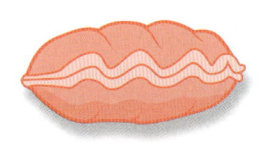

Revisiting the Text

Future Vocabulary

- Say *In this picture, the fish is beside the shell. Could the fish be on top of the shell?* (yes) *Where else could the fish be?* (behind the shell) Discuss how some words describe where two things are, compared to each other. Brainstorm more of these positional words with children, such as *left, right, above, below,* and *underneath.*

- Explain that this shell has two parts, a top and a bottom.

Now revisit pages 10–11

During Reading

Book Talk

- Read the sentence on page 10. Have children locate the word *diver* on this page. Say *A diver is a person who stays underwater for a long time. A diver breathes air from a tank.*

- **Comprehension Strategy** Ask *Is the diver in the picture supposed to be a real person?* (no) *How do you know?* (It's too small; it's *inside* the bowl with the fish.)

Turn to page 12 – Book Talk

My little fish is beside the diver.

Revisiting the Text

Future Vocabulary

- Say *In this picture, the fish is beside the diver. Could the fish be on top of the diver?* (yes) Discuss multiple meanings of *top*. (lid; the best, as in "top dog" or "top player")

- Ask *Did you know that there is a toy called a top? Do you know how a top moves?* (It spins.) If possible, show children a top and how it works.

Now revisit pages 12–13

11

During Reading

Book Talk
- Read the sentence on page 12. Have children locate the word *beside* on this page.

Turn to page 14 — Book Talk

My little fish is beside the cave.

Revisiting the Text

Future Vocabulary

- Ask children where they might find a real cave. (in a mountain, in the woods) Ask *What kind of material is a cave made out of?* (rock, soil) *Do you think this kind of material would float or sink?* (sink)

Now revisit pages 14–15

During Reading

Book Talk

- Ask children if they have any more questions about the book to write in the Questions and Answers Chart.

Turn to page 16 – Book Talk

My little fish is . . .

Revisiting the Text

Future Vocabulary
- **Comprehension Strategy** Ask *Where is the gold fish now?* (inside the cave) *How do you know?* (the way the lines are drawn in the picture)

Go to page T5 – Revisiting the Text

15

During Reading

Book Talk
- Leave this page for children to discover on their own when they read the book individually.

Individual Reading
Have each child read the entire book at his or her own pace while remaining in the group.

Go to page T5 – Revisiting the Text

inside the cave.

16

During independent work time, children can read the online book at:
www.rigbyflyingcolors.com

16

Revisiting the Text

Future Vocabulary
- Use the notes on the right-hand pages to develop oral vocabulary that goes beyond the text. These vocabulary words first appear in future texts. These words are: *top*, *gold*, and *float*.

Turn back to page 1

Reading Vocabulary Review
Activity Sheet: Sentence Maker

- Write these words on the board: *beside*, *inside*, and *diver*. Ask *What is the difference between* beside *and* inside*?*
- Have children complete the Sentence Maker using the word *inside*.

Comprehension Strategy Review
Use Interactive Modeling Card: Questions and Answers Chart

- Discuss *My Little Fish*. Together complete the Questions and Answers Chart.
- Refer to the text and use the discussion questions on page T7 to review drawing conclusions with children as they answer the questions on the chart.

Phonics Review
- Have children skim the book for words that begin or end with *sh*. *(fish, shell)*
- Review the lists of /sh/ words children brainstormed earlier. Have children use one or two of the words on the list in a sentence.

Fluency Review
- Partner children and have them take turns reading page 16, emphasizing the word *inside*.
- Have children read the sentence on page 2, emphasizing a different word each time. Discuss how emphasis can change the way you think about what is read.

Reading-Writing Connection
Activity Sheet: Questions and Answers Chart

To assist children with linking reading and writing:
- Use the Questions and Answers Chart to model writing about a pet. Ask *If you could have any pet you wanted, what would it be? How would you care for it?*
- Have children complete and use the Questions and Answers Chart to write about their own pets or a pet they would like to have.

T5

4 Assessment

Assessing Future Vocabulary

Work with each child individually. Ask questions that elicit each child's understanding of the Future Vocabulary words. Note each child's responses:

- What do people often have on top of their bed?
- What is something made of gold?
- What floats on the water?

Assessing Comprehension Strategy

Work with each child individually. Note each child's understanding of drawing conclusions:

- Where does the fish live?
- What does the fish eat?
- Who takes care of the fish?
- Was each child able to draw reasonable conclusions based on his or her prior knowledge and the text and illustrations in *My Little Fish*?

Assessing Phonics

Work with each child individually. Have each child read the words on the lists of /sh/ words or the following words: *fish, shell, dash,* and *short.* Note each child's responses for understanding initial and final /sh/:

- Did each child correctly pronounce /sh/ at the beginning or end of each word?
- Did each child make the connection between /sh/ and the consonant blend *sh*?

Assessing Fluency

Have each child read page 16 to you. Note each child's understanding of emphasizing words in boldfaced type to inform expression:

- Was each child able to decode and accurately read the reading vocabulary word *inside*?
- Did each child emphasize the word in boldfaced type?

Interactive Modeling Cards

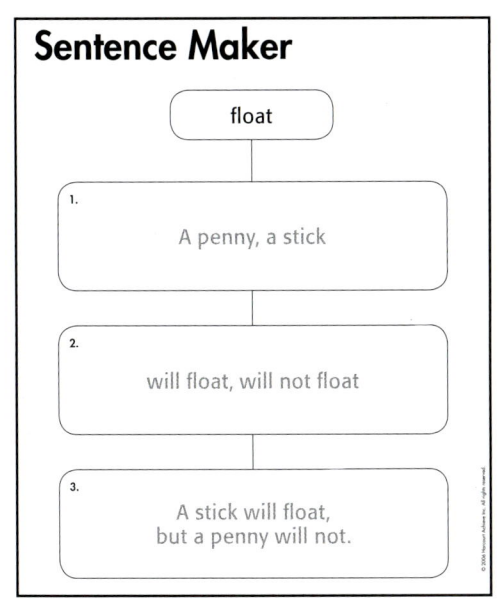

Sentence Maker

float

1. A penny, a stick

2. will float, will not float

3. A stick will float, but a penny will not.

Directions: With children, fill in the Sentence Maker using the word *float*.

Questions and Answers Chart

Title: _My Little Fish_
Topic: _What the fish will do_

Questions	Answers
Where does the fish go after it is beside the boat?	It swims beside the plant.
Did the shell open up?	No, the shell stayed closed.

Directions: With children, fill in the Questions and Answers Chart for *My Little Fish*.

Discussion Questions

- What color is the fish? (Literal)
- Why is the fish bowl clear? (Critical Thinking)
- How did the things get inside the fish bowl? (Inferential)

Activity Sheets

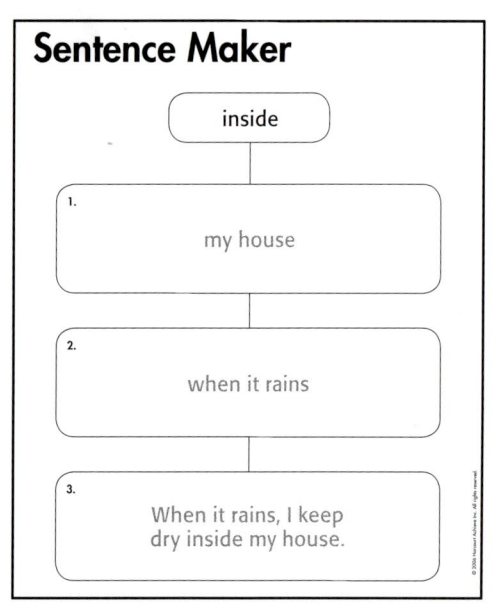

Sentence Maker

inside

1. my house

2. when it rains

3. When it rains, I keep dry inside my house.

Directions: Have children fill in the Sentence Maker using *inside*.

Questions and Answers Chart

Title: *My Little Fish*
Topic: What makes a good pet

Questions	Answers
Why is a fish a good pet?	easy to take care of, small
Why is a hamster a good pet?	does tricks, stays in a cage
Why is a horse a good pet?	A horse is too big to be a good pet!

Directions: Have children, independently or with a partner, fill in the Questions and Answers Chart about their pets or a pet they would like to have. Optional: On a separate sheet of paper, have children draw a picture of their real or imaginary pet and write about how they would take care of it.